This Crosswords Puzzle Book Belongs To:

_____

Black Heroines Crosswords #1

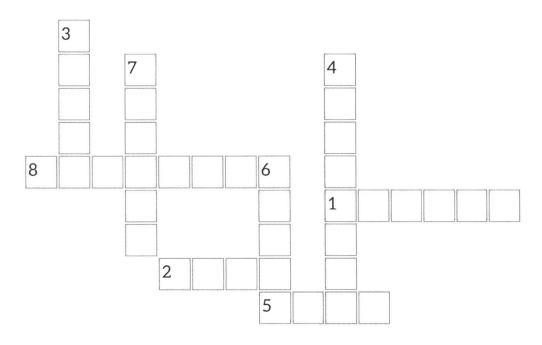

Across

[1] Harriet ___ was an abolitionist and conductor on the Underground Railroad.

[2] ___ Parks was a civil rights activist known for refusing to give up her seat on a bus.

[5] ___ Angelou was a celebrated poet, memoirist, and civil rights activist.

[8] Shirley ___ was the first black woman elected to the United States Congress.

Down

[3] Sojourner ___ was an abolitionist and women's rights activist.

[4] Phillis ___ was the first published African-American female poet.

[6] ___ C.J. Walker was the female self-made millionaire in America--a beauty and hair care mogul.

[7] ___ Coleman was the first African-American woman to hold a pilot's license.

Black Heroines Crosswords #1 - Solution

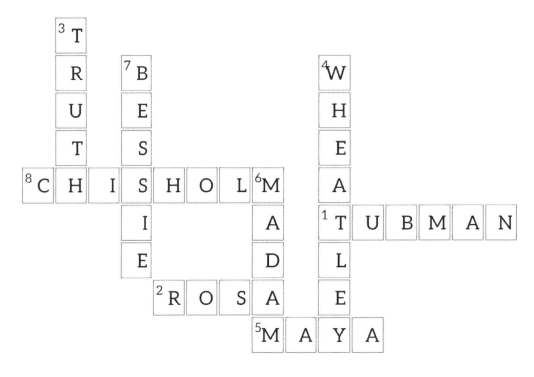

Across

[1] Harriet ___ was an abolitionist and conductor on the Underground Railroad.

[2] ___ Parks was a civil rights activist known for refusing to give up her seat on a bus.

[5] ___ Angelou was a celebrated poet, memoirist, and civil rights activist.

[8] Shirley ___ was the first black woman elected to the United States Congress.

Down

[3] Sojourner ___ was an abolitionist and women's rights activist.

[4] Phillis ___ was the first published African-American female poet.

[6] ___ C.J. Walker was the female self-made millionaire in America--a beauty and hair care mogul.

[7] ___ Coleman was the first African-American woman to hold a pilot's license.

Black Heroines Crosswords #2

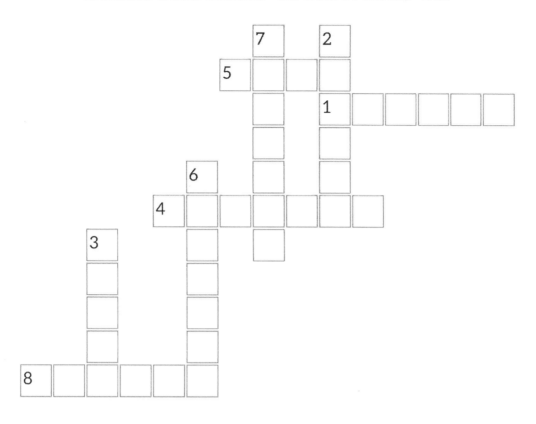

Across

[1] ___ Holiday was a Legendary jazz singer.

[4] Mary McLeod ___ was an educator, stateswoman, and civil rights activist.

[5] ___ Morrison was a Nobel Prize-winning novelist.

[8] ___ Anderson was a celebrated contralto singer and the first black person to perform at the Metropolitan Opera.

Down

[2] Althea ___ was the first black tennis player to compete at Wimbledon.

[3] Josephine ___ was an internationally acclaimed singer, dancer, and spy during WWII.

[6] Mae ___ is the first African-American female astronaut.

[7] ___ Dandridge was the first African-American actress nominated for an Academy Award for Best Actress.

Black Heroines Crosswords #2 - Solution

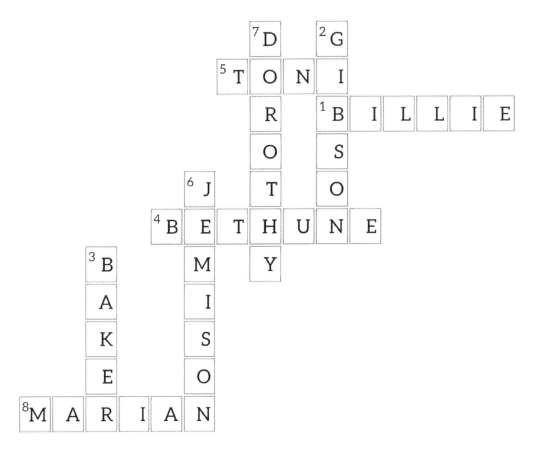

Across

[1] ___ Holiday was a Legendary jazz singer.

[4] Mary McLeod ___ was an educator, stateswoman, and civil rights activist.

[5] ___ Morrison was a Nobel Prize-winning novelist.

[8] ___ Anderson was a celebrated contralto singer and the first black person to perform at the Metropolitan Opera.

Down

[2] Althea ___ was the first black tennis player to compete at Wimbledon.

[3] Josephine ___ was an internationally acclaimed singer, dancer, and spy during WWII.

[6] Mae ___ is the first African-American female astronaut.

[7] ___ Dandridge was the first African-American actress nominated for an Academy Award for Best Actress.

Black Women Icons Crosswords #3

Across

[3] Oprah ____ is a media mogul, actress, and philanthropist.

[5] Angela ___ is a political activist, scholar, and author.

[7] ___ Scott King was the wife of Martin Luther King Jr.

Down

[1] Ida B. ___ was a journalist and abolitionist who led an anti-lynching crusade in the U.S.

[2] ___ Lou Hamer played a vital role in organizing Mississippi's Freedom Summer.

[4] Gwendolyn ___ was a Pulitzer Prize-winning poet and educator.

[6] ___ Lorde was a poet, writer, and civil rights activist.

[8] ___ Neale Hurston was an author and anthropologist.

Black Women Icons Crosswords #3 - Solution

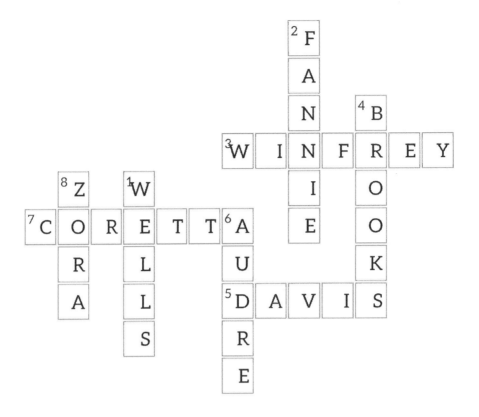

Across

[3] Oprah ___ is a media mogul, actress, and philanthropist.

[5] Angela ___ is a political activist, scholar, and author.

[7] ___ Scott King was the wife of Martin Luther King Jr.

Down

[1] Ida B. ___ was a journalist and abolitionist who led an anti-lynching crusade in the U.S.

[2] ___ Lou Hamer played a vital role in organizing Mississippi's Freedom Summer.

[4] Gwendolyn ___ was a Pulitzer Prize-winning poet and educator.

[6] ___ Lorde was a poet, writer, and civil rights activist.

[8] ___ Neale Hurston was an author and anthropologist.

Black Women Icons Crosswords #4

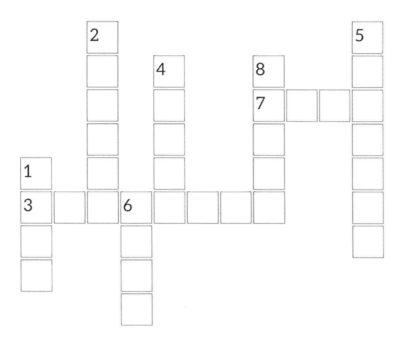

Across

[3] ___ Hansberry was a playwright best known for "A Raisin in the Sun."

[7] ___ Simmons was the first black president of an Ivy League institution.

Down

[1] ___ Fitzgerald was a renowned jazz singer, the "First Lady of Song."

[2] Octavia ___ was an acclaimed science fiction writer.

[4] ___ Rudolph was an Olympic champion in track and field.

[5] Katherine ___ was a NASA mathematician profiled in the movie "Hidden Figures."

[6] ___ Bridges is the first African-American child to integrate into an all-white school in the South.

[8] Florence ___ was the First African-American woman recognized as a symphonic composer.

Black Women Icons Crosswords #4 - Solution

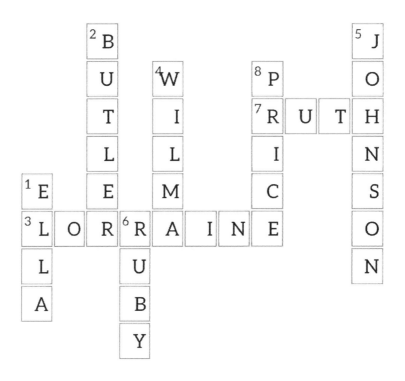

Across

[3] ___ Hansberry was a playwright best known for "A Raisin in the Sun."

[7] ___ Simmons was the first black president of an Ivy League institution.

Down

[1] ___ Fitzgerald was a renowned jazz singer, the "First Lady of Song."

[2] Octavia ___ was an acclaimed science fiction writer.

[4] ___ Rudolph was an Olympic champion in track and field.

[5] Katherine ___ was a NASA mathematician profiled in the movie "Hidden Figures."

[6] ___ Bridges is the first African-American child to integrate into an all-white school in the South.

[8] Florence ___ was the First African-American woman recognized as a symphonic

Black Heroines in Every Clue #5

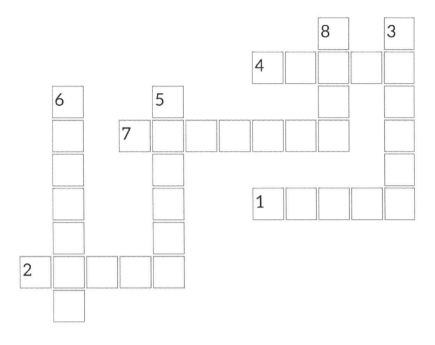

Across

[1] ___ Walker is the Pulitzer Prize-winning author of "The Color Purple."

[2] ___ Bumbry was an acclaimed opera singer.

[4] ___ Ringgold was an artist best known for narrative quilts.

[7] ___ Lee Crumpler was the first Black American woman to get a medical degree in the U.S.

Down

[3] Sister Rosetta __ was a gospel singer and major early rock & roll influence.

[5] __ Norman was an internationally acclaimed opera vocalist.

[6] __ Jordan was the first Southern African-American U.S. Congresswoman.

[8] __ Simone was a passionate singer, songwriter, and civil rights activist.

Black Heroines in Every Clue #5 - Solution

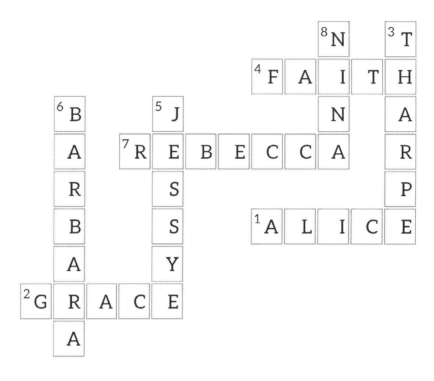

Across

[1] ___ Walker is the Pulitzer Prize-winning author of "The Color Purple."

[2] ___ Bumbry was an acclaimed opera singer.

[4] ___ Ringgold was an artist best known for narrative quilts.

[7] ___ Lee Crumpler was the first Black American woman to get a medical degree in the U.S.

Down

[3] Sister Rosetta ___ was a gospel singer and major early rock & roll influence.

[5] ___ Norman was an internationally acclaimed opera vocalist.

[6] ___ Jordan was the first Southern African-American U.S. Congresswoman.

[8] ___ Simone was a passionate singer, songwriter, and civil rights activist.

Black Heroines in Every Clue #6

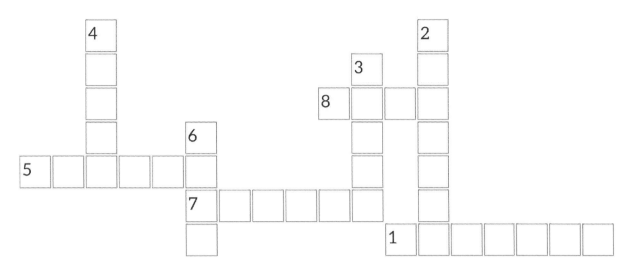

Across

[1] Beyonce ___ is a famous international singer, actress, and entrepreneur.

[5] ___ Franklin was the "Queen of Soul" and a famous singer.

[7] ___ Williams is a famous Tennis champion.

[8] Condoleezza ___ was the first Black female U.S. Secretary of State.

Down

[2] Marian Wright ___ was the founder of the Children's Defense Fund.

[3] ___ Davis is an Award-winning actress.

[4] Tarana ___ is an activist and founder of the #MeToo movement.

[6] Diane ___ was a civil rights and peace activist.

Black Heroines in Every Clue #6 - Solution

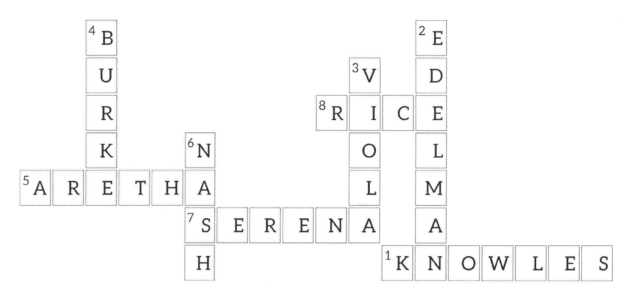

Across

[1] Beyonce ___ is a famous international singer, actress, and entrepreneur.

[5] ___ Franklin was the "Queen of Soul" and a famous singer.

[7] ___ Williams is a famous Tennis champion.

[8] Condoleezza ___ was the first Black female U.S. Secretary of State.

Down

[2] Marian Wright ___ was the founder of the Children's Defense Fund.

[3] ___ Davis is an Award-winning actress.

[4] Tarana ___ is an activist and founder of the #MeToo movement.

[6] Diane ___ was a civil rights and peace activist.

Legends in Every Square #7

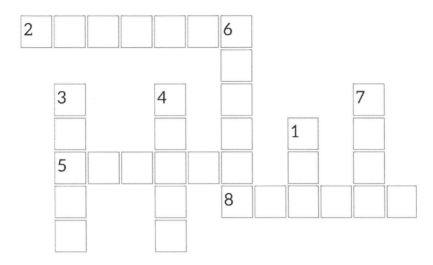

Across

[2] Chimamanda Ngozi ___ is a famous Nigerian novelist and feminist speaker.

[5] Afeni ___ was a Black political activist and the mother of Tupac Shakur.

[8] ___ Abrams is a political leader and voting rights activist.

Down

[1] ___ DuVernay is a writer, film director, and producer.

[3] Cicely___ was a trailblazing actress best known for strong, resilient Black women roles.

[4] ___ Giovanni was a Black poet, writer, commentator, and educator who used her work to promote civil rights.

[6] Joycelyn ___ was the first African-American U.S. Surgeon General.

[7] ___ Newsome is a black activist known for taking down the Confederate flag from South Carolina's statehouse.

Legends in Every Square #7 - Solution

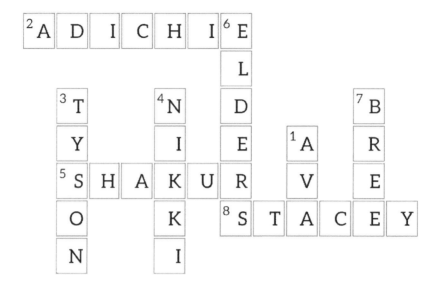

Across

[2] Chimamanda Ngozi ___ is a famous Nigerian novelist and feminist speaker.

[5] Afeni ___ was a Black political activist and the mother of Tupac Shakur.

[8] ___ Abrams is a political leader and voting rights activist.

Down

[1] ___ DuVernay is a writer, film director, and producer.

[3] Cicely___ was a trailblazing actress best known for strong, resilient Black women roles.

[4] ___ Giovanni was a Black poet, writer, commentator, and educator who used her work to promote civil rights.

[6] Joycelyn ___ was the first African-American U.S. Surgeon General.

[7] ___ Newsome is a black activist known for taking down the Confederate flag from South Carolina's statehouse.

Legends in Every Square #8

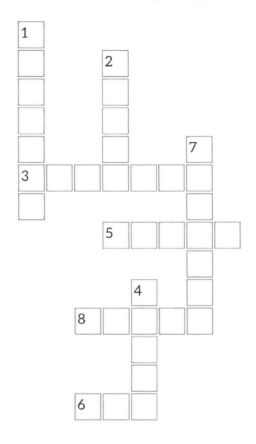

Across

[3] ___ is a global pop star and Black businesswoman.

[5] Daisy ___ was a civil rights activist and newspaper publisher.

[6] Roxane ___ is a writer, professor, and commentator.

[8] Leontyne ___ is the first Black American to receive international fame as a soprano opera singer.

Down

[1] ___ Maathai was the first African Nobel Prize-winning environmental activist.

[2] Michelle ___ was the first Black First Lady of the United States.

[4] ___ Copeland is the first Black American female principal dancer at the American Ballet Theatre.

[7] ___ Monae is a famous Black singer, rapper, songwriter, and actress.

Legends in Every Square #8 - Solution

Across

[3] ___ is a global pop star and Black businesswoman.

[5] Daisy ___ was a civil rights activist and newspaper publisher.

[6] Roxane ___ is a writer, professor, and commentator.

[8] Leontyne ___ is the first Black American to receive international fame as a soprano opera singer.

Down

[1] ___ Maathai was the first African Nobel Prize-winning environmental activist.

[2] Michelle ___ was the first Black First Lady of the United States.

[4] ___ Copeland is the first Black American female principal dancer at the American Ballet Theatre.

[7] ___ Monae is a famous Black singer, rapper, songwriter, and actress.

Remarkable Black Women Crosswords #9

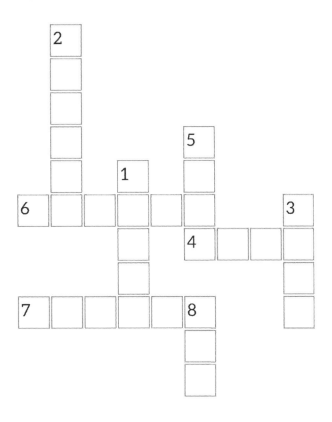

Across

[4] ___ Shahidi is an activist and actress famous for her role in the "Black-ish" TV show.

[6] Gloria ___ was an iconic disco-era singer known for "I Will Survive."

[7] ___ Nyongo is a Mexican-Kenyan Oscar-winning actress famous for her "Black Panther" role.

Down

[1] ___ Okorafor is an award-winning Nigerian-American science fiction and fantasy writer.

[2] ___ Mallory is a social justice leader who was the youngest ever National Action Network Executive Director.

[3] ___ was the first Black woman to run for U.S. Vice President (1952).

[5] ___ Church Terrell was an early civil rights activist and suffragist.

[8] ___ Ashwood Garvey was a Pan-African activist and first wife of Marcus Garvey.

Remarkable Black Women Crosswords #9 - Solution

Across

[4] ___ Shahidi is an activist and actress famous for her role in the "Black-ish" TV show.

[6] Gloria ___ was an iconic disco-era singer known for "I Will Survive."

[7] ___ Nyongo is a Mexican-Kenyan Oscar-winning actress famous for her "Black Panther" role.

Down

[1] ___ Okorafor is an award-winning Nigerian-American science fiction and fantasy writer.

[2] ___ Mallory is a social justice leader who was the youngest ever National Action Network Executive Director.

[3] ___ was the first Black woman to run for U.S. Vice President (1952).

[5] ___ Church Terrell was an early civil rights activist and suffragist.

[8] ___ Ashwood Garvey was a Pan-African activist and first wife of Marcus Garvey.

Remarkable Black Women Crosswords #10

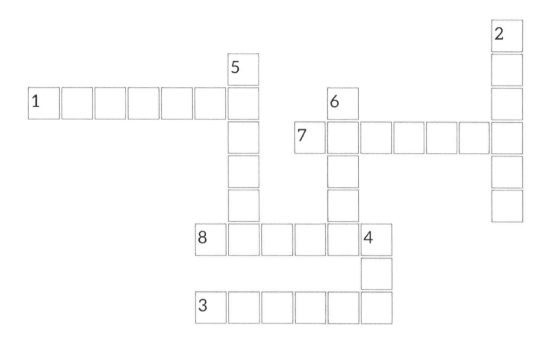

Across

[1] Queen ___ is a Black-American woman rapper, singer, and actress.

[3] ___ McDaniel was the first Black American woman to win the coveted Oscar Award.

[7] ___ Kincaid is a Caribbean-American novelist and essayist about family relationships.

[8] Candace ___ is a professional basketball player who was the first woman to dunk in an NCAA game.

Down

[2] ___ Harris is the first Black-American and female U.S. Vice President.

[4] Issa ___ is a Black American activist, actress, writer, and producer.

[5] ___ Rhimes is an African-American TV producer and screenwriter famous for "Grey's Anatomy."

[6] ___ Smith is a Black British novelist and essayist who writes about race and culture.

Remarkable Black Women Crosswords #10 - Solution

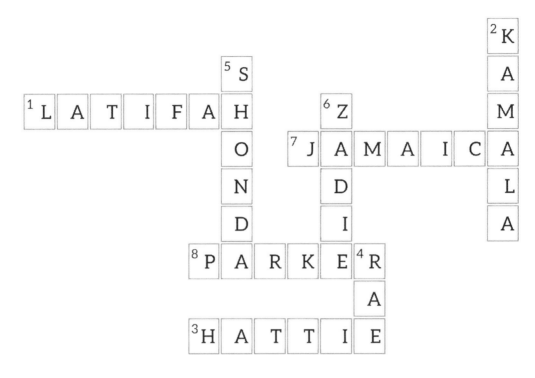

Across

[1] Queen __ is a Black-American woman rapper, singer, and actress.

[3] ___ McDaniel was the first Black American woman to win the coveted Oscar Award.

[7] __ Kincaid is a Caribbean-American novelist and essayist about family relationships.

[8] Candace __ is a professional basketball player who was the first woman to dunk in an NCAA game.

Down

[2] ___ Harris is the first Black-American and female U.S. Vice President.

[4] Issa __ is a Black American activist, actress, writer, and producer.

[5] ___ Rhimes is an African-American TV producer and screenwriter famous for "Grey's Anatomy."

[6] __ Smith is a Black British novelist and essayist who writes about race and culture.

Celebrating Black Women of Worth #11

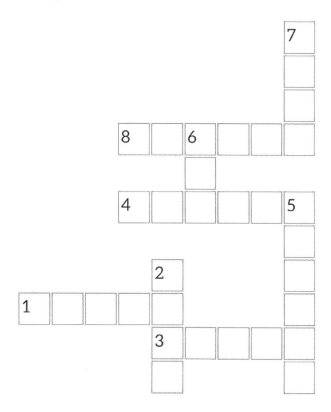

Across

[1] ___ La Negra is a singer, reality TV star, and Afro-Latina advocate.

[3] ___ Thompson is a Black actress famous for her role in "Creed".

[4] ___ Waters is a U.S. Congresswoman and the longest serving of the black women in Congress.

[8] ___ Joyner-Kersee won six Olympic medals in track and field events.

Down

[2] Patricia ___ was the first Black woman to receive a medical patent in the U.S. for her laser cataract surgery invention.

[5] ___ Palcy is a filmmaker and the first black woman to direct a film produced by a major Hollywood studio.

[6] Laverne ___ is a transgender actress and LGBTQ+ advocate.

[7] Rita ___ is the second Black American to receive the Pulitzer Prize for Poetry.

Celebrating Black Women of Worth #11 - Solution

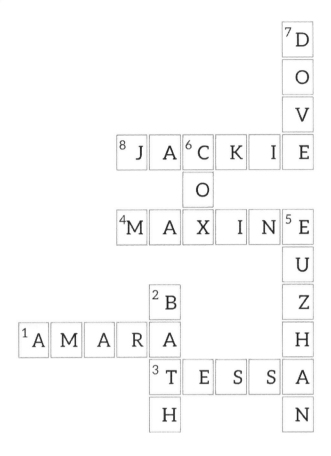

Across

[1] ___ La Negra is a singer, reality TV star, and Afro-Latina advocate.

[3] ___ Thompson is a Black actress famous for her role in "Creed".

[4] ___ Waters is a U.S. Congresswoman and the longest serving of the black women in Congress.

[8] ___ Joyner-Kersee won six Olympic medals in track and field events.

Down

[2] Patricia ___ was the first Black woman to receive a medical patent in the U.S. for her laser cataract surgery invention.

[5] ___ Palcy is a filmmaker and the first black woman to direct a film produced by a major Hollywood studio.

[6] Laverne ___ is a transgender actress and LGBTQ+ advocate.

[7] Rita ___ is the second Black American to receive the Pulitzer Prize for Poetry.

Celebrating Black Women of Worth #12

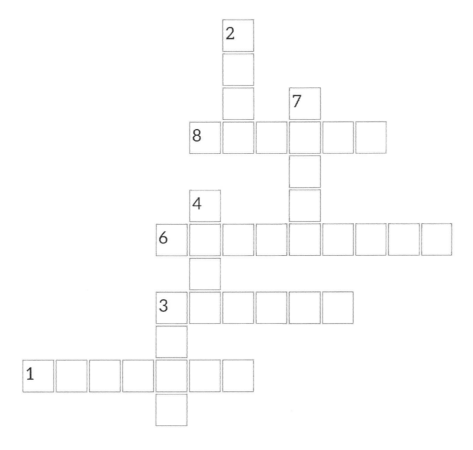

Across

[1] Mary Eliza ___ was the first Black professionally trained nurse in the U.S.

[3] ___ Helen Burroughs founded The National Trade and Professional School for Women and Girls.

[6] ___ Taylor-Greensfield was touted worldwide as the most gifted vocalist with a wide range covering 27 notes.

[8] Mary ___ was a pioneer, freight hauler, and the second woman to drive a U.S. Mail Coach.

Down

[2] Yvonne ___ is a Nigerian-American actress and comedian.

[3] ___ Mae McKinney was the first Black female motion picture star.

[4] ___ Philips Stewart was a nationally known Black woman pharmacist.

[7] ___ brown was the first black woman to cross the plains during the Colorado Gold Rush.

Celebrating Black Women of Worth #12 - Solution

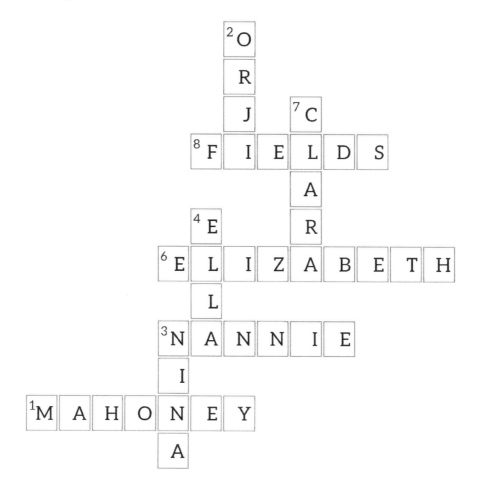

Across

[1] Mary Eliza ___ was the first Black professionally trained nurse in the U.S.

[3] ___ Helen Burroughs founded The National Trade and Professional School for Women and Girls.

[6] ___ Taylor-Greensfield was touted worldwide as the most gifted vocalist with a wide range covering 27 notes.

[8] Mary ___ was a pioneer, freight hauler, and the second woman to drive a U.S. Mail Coach.

Down

[2] Yvonne ___ is a Nigerian-American actress and comedian.

[3] ___ Mae McKinney was the first Black female motion picture star.

[4] ___ Philips Stewart was a nationally known Black woman pharmacist.

[7] ___ brown was the first black woman to cross the plains during the Colorado Gold Rush.

Shining Stars Crosswords #13

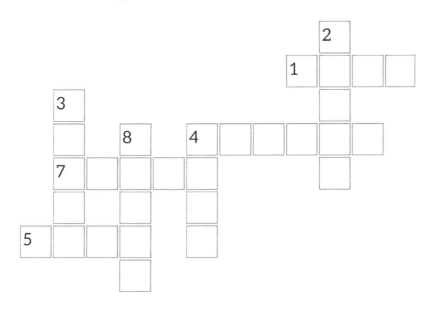

Across

[1] ___ Augustine was the first Black woman in the Canadian House of Commons.

[4] ___ Allen is a famous Black actress, dancer, choreographer, and director.

[5] MC ___, was the first Black female artist to perform Hip Hop at the White House.

[7] ___ J. Mohammed is a British Nigerian diplomat and the fifth Deputy Secretary-General of the United Nations.

Down

[2] Allyson ___ is the most decorated female Olympian in track and field.

[3] ___ Chapman is a Black American singer and songwriter.

[4] ___ was the first Black American woman to get a wide theatrical release of a feature film.

[8] Simone ___ is a World champion Black gymnast with 25 World Championship medals.

Shining Stars Crosswords #13 - Solution

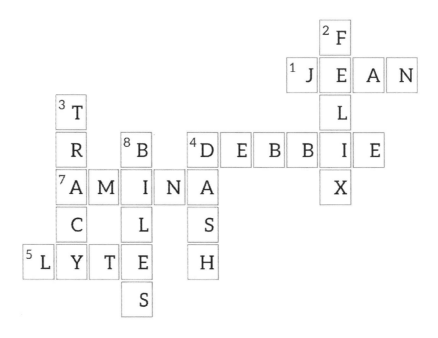

Across

[1] __ Augustine was the first Black woman in the Canadian House of Commons.

[4] __ Allen is a famous Black actress, dancer, choreographer, and director.

[5] MC __, was the first Black female artist to perform Hip Hop at the White House.

[7] __ J. Mohammed is a British Nigerian diplomat and the fifth Deputy Secretary-General of the United Nations.

Down

[2] Allyson __ is the most decorated female Olympian in track and field.

[3] ___ Chapman is a Black American singer and songwriter.

[4] __ was the first Black American woman to get a wide theatrical release of a feature film.

[8] Simone __ is a World champion Black gymnast with 25 World Championship medals.

Shining Stars Crosswords #14

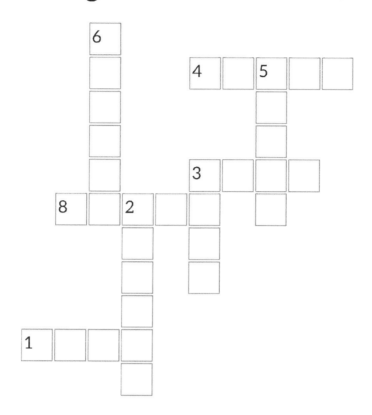

Across

[1] ___ Banks is a Black supermodel, television host, and businesswoman.

[3] Beverly ___ founded "Black Girls Rock!" a mentorship program for young women.

[4] Gabrielle ___ is a Black actress and activist.

[8] ___ Van Brittan Brown, a Black woman, invented the first home security system.

Down

[2] Phylicia ___ was the first Black American actress to receive a Tony Award for Best Actress.

[3] ___ Hooks was a Black Author, feminist, and social critic who wrote about race, gender, and class.

[5] __ Perry is a scholar, writer, and historian of law, race, and culture.

[6] Miriam ___ is a South African singer and anti-apartheid activist.

Shining Stars Crosswords #14 - Solution

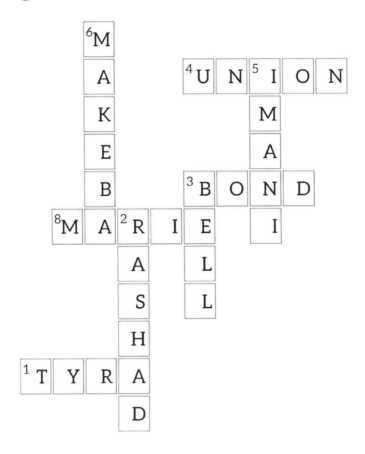

Across

[1] ___ Banks is a Black supermodel, television host, and businesswoman.

[3] Beverly ___ founded "Black Girls Rock!" a mentorship program for young women.

[4] Gabrielle ___ is a Black actress and activist.

[8] ___ Van Brittan Brown, a Black woman, invented the first home security system.

Down

[2] Phylicia ___ was the first Black American actress to receive a Tony Award for Best Actress.

[3] ___ Hooks was a Black Author, feminist, and social critic who wrote about race, gender, and class.

[5] _ Perry is a scholar, writer, and historian of law, race, and culture.

[6] Miriam ___ is a South African singer and anti-apartheid activist.

Women Who Paved Our Way #15

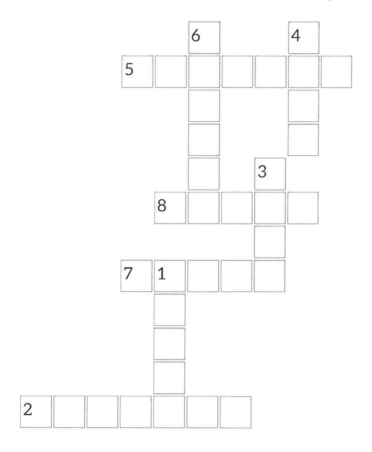

Across

[2] Winnie ___, was a South African anti-apartheid activist and politician.

[5] ___ Rankine is a Jamaican-born poet and essayist.

[7] ___ Jackson is a famous singer, songwriter, actress, and dancer.

[8] Edmonia ___ was the African American and Native American woman to achieve international recognition as a sculptor.

Down

[1] ___ Thomas is a Black young adult author who wrote "The Hate U Give."

[3] Eartha ___ was a famous Black American singer, actress, and dancer with a distinctive style and voice.

[4] Anita ___ is a law professor, educator, and women's rights advocate.

[6] ___ Lena Walker was the first Black-American woman to charter a bank in the U.S.

Women Who Paved Our Way #15 - Solution

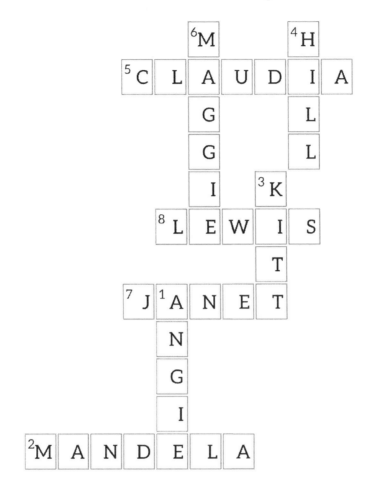

Across

[2] Winnie ___, was a South African anti-apartheid activist and politician.

[5] ___ Rankine is a Jamaican-born poet and essayist.

[7] ___ Jackson is a famous singer, songwriter, actress, and dancer.

[8] Edmonia ___ was the African American and Native American woman to achieve international recognition as a sculptor.

Down

[1] ___ Thomas is a Black young adult author who wrote "The Hate U Give."

[3] Eartha ___ was a famous Black American singer, actress, and dancer with a distinctive style and voice.

[4] Anita ___ is a law professor, educator, and women's rights advocate.

[6] ___ Lena Walker was the first Black-American woman to charter a bank in the U.S.

Women Who Paved Our Way #16

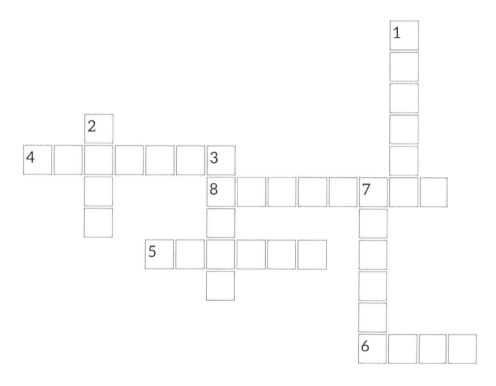

Across

[4] __ Ellen Watkins Harper was the first African-American to publish a short story.

[5] __ Jones (Baby Esther) was an entertainer and the model for the "Betty Boop" character.

[6] __ Keita Jemisin is a celebrated Black science fiction and fantasy author.

[8] Kimberle __ is a civil rights advocate and a leading scholar of critical race theory.

Down

[1] ___ Mizanekristos is an African-American singer and songwriter.

[2] __ Hopkinson is a Jamaican-born Canadian award-winning science fiction writer and editor.

[3] Jill __ is an inspiring African-American female poet, singer, songwriter, and actress.

[7] Jennifer __ was the first African-American singer on the "Vogue" magazine cover.

Women Who Paved Our Way #16 - Solution

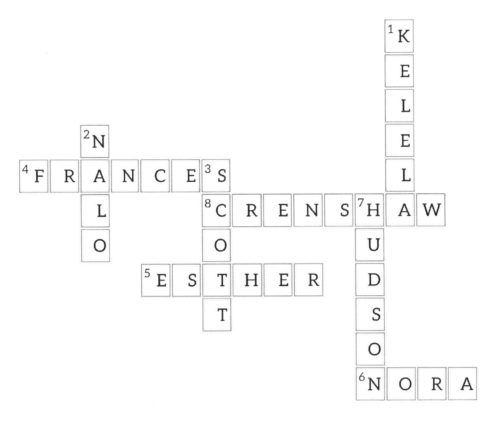

Across

[4] __ Ellen Watkins Harper was the first African-American to publish a short story.

[5] __ Jones (Baby Esther) was an entertainer and the model for the "Betty Boop" character.

[6] __ Keita Jemisin is a celebrated Black science fiction and fantasy author.

[8] Kimberle __ is a civil rights advocate and a leading scholar of critical race theory.

Down

[1] ___ Mizanekristos is an African-American singer and songwriter.

[2] __ Hopkinson is a Jamaican-born Canadian award-winning science fiction writer and editor.

[3] Jill __ is an inspiring African-American female poet, singer, songwriter, and actress.

[7] Jennifer __ was the first African-American singer on the "Vogue" magazine cover.

Black Women of Greatness and Legacy #17

Across

[2] ___ Loroupe is a Kenyan long-distance track and road runner and the first African woman to win the New York Marathon.

[3] Queen ___ was the 17th-century queen of the Ndongo and Matamba Kingdoms (modern-day Angola).

[6] Solange ____ is a fashion model, singer, songwriter, and visual artist.

[8] Marjorie ___ invented the Permanent Wave Machine for hairstyles.

Down

[1] ___ Spencer is a famous actress best known for her "The Help" role.

[4] ___ Ransome-Kuti was a Nigerian educator and women's rights activist.

[5] ___ Cooper Cafritz was an educator, art collector, and Duke Ellington School of the Arts founder.

[7] ___ Campbell is a supermodel and the first black woman to appear on the covers of Time and Vogue France.

Black Women of Greatness and Legacy #17 - Solution

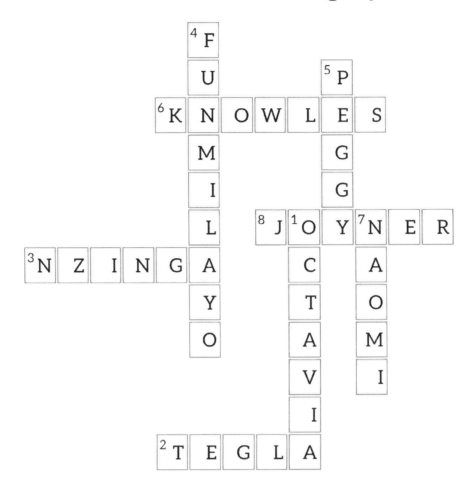

Across

[2] ___ Loroupe is a Kenyan long-distance track and road runner and the first African woman to win the New York Marathon.

[3] Queen ___ was the 17th-century queen of the Ndongo and Matamba Kingdoms (modern-day Angola).

[6] Solange ___ is a fashion model, singer, songwriter, and visual artist.

[8] Marjorie ___ invented the Permanent Wave Machine for hairstyles.

Down

[1] ___ Spencer is a famous actress best known for her "The Help" role.

[4] ___ Ransome-Kuti was a Nigerian educator and women's rights activist.

[5] ___ Cooper Cafritz was an educator, art collector, and Duke Ellington School of the Arts founder.

[7] ___ Campbell is a supermodel and the first black woman to appear on the covers of Time and Vogue France.

Black Women of Greatness and Legacy #18

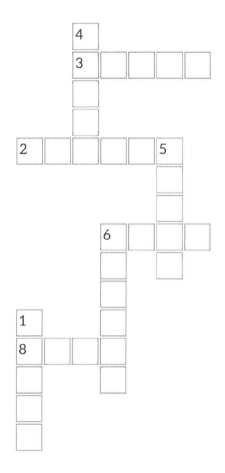

Across

[2] Rosalind ___ is the COO of Starbucks and former CEO of Sam's Club.

[3] Attica ___ is a Black novelist and writer for television and film.

[6] Regina ___ , Award-winning actress and director considered one of the 100 most influential people in the world.

[8] ___ Taylor Morton was the first and only Black American to serve as U.S. Treasurer.

Down

[1] ___ Hughes is a media proprietor and the second-richest Black woman in the U.S.

[4] ___ Dunbar-Nelson was a Black poet, journalist, and political activist.

[5] Sylvia ___ is a music industry executive and the chair and CEO of Epic Records.

[6] Normani ___ is a Black American singer and dancer.

Black Women of Greatness and Legacy #18 - Solution

Across

[2] Rosalind ___ is the COO of Starbucks and former CEO of Sam's Club.

[3] Attica ___ is a Black novelist and writer for television and film.

[6] Regina ___ , Award-winning actress and director considered one of the 100 most influential people in the world.

[8] ___ Taylor Morton was the first and only Black American to serve as U.S. Treasurer.

Down

[1] ___ Hughes is a media proprietor and the second-richest Black woman in the U.S.

[4] ___ Dunbar-Nelson was a Black poet, journalist, and political activist.

[5] Sylvia ___ is a music industry executive and the chair and CEO of Epic Records.

[6] Normani ___ is a Black American singer and dancer.

Black Pearls Crosswords #19

Across

[1] __ Mallory was a civil rights activist focused on school desegregation.

[5] __ Jackson was touted as the "Queen of Gospel" singer.

[6] Mary Ann Shadd __ was the first Black newspaperwoman in North America.

[8] __Bird Fauset was the first Black woman state legislator in the U.S.

Down

[2] __ Bland was a Black American activist whose death in custody sparked protests.

[3] Ursula ___ is the former CEO of Xerox and the first Black woman CEO of a Fortune 500 company.

[4] __ Horne was a famous Black American singer, dancer, actress, and civil rights activist.

[7] Ellen __ was a famous "master of disguise" who escaped slavery disguised as a respectable white man.

Black Pearls Crosswords #19 - Solution

Across

[1] ___ Mallory was a civil rights activist focused on school desegregation.

[5] ___ Jackson was touted as the "Queen of Gospel" singer.

[6] Mary Ann Shadd ___ was the first Black newspaperwoman in North America.

[8] ___Bird Fauset was the first Black woman state legislator in the U.S.

Down

[2] ___ Bland was a Black American activist whose death in custody sparked protests.

[3] Ursula ___ is the former CEO of Xerox and the first Black woman CEO of a Fortune 500 company.

[4] ___ Horne was a famous Black American singer, dancer, actress, and civil rights activist.

[7] Ellen ___ was a famous "master of disguise" who escaped slavery disguised as a respectable white man.

Black Pearls Crosswords #20

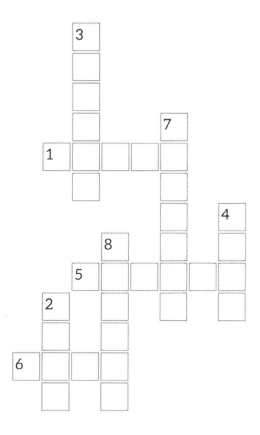

Across

[1] ___ Abbott, first black woman elected to the UK Parliament.

[5] Thelma ___, a museum director and art curator for artists of African descent.

[6] ___ Adu Nigerian-born iconic singer and songwriter.

Down

[2] Chaka ___, a Black singer who won 10 Grammy Awards.

[3] ___Garza, co-founder of "Black Lives Matter."

[4] ___ Braxton, a Black singer who won many Grammy Awards.

[7] ___ Hobson, a Black Businesswoman, investor, and chair of Starbucks.

[8] Mary ___, a former enslaved secret spy for the Union in the Civil War.

Black Pearls Crosswords #20 - Solution

Across

[1] ___ Abbott, first black woman elected to the UK Parliament.

[5] Thelma ___, a museum director and art curator for artists of African descent.

[6] ___ Adu Nigerian-born iconic singer and songwriter.

Down

[2] Chaka ___, a Black singer who won 10 Grammy Awards.

[3] ___Garza, co-founder of "Black Lives Matter."

[4] ___ Braxton, a Black singer who won many Grammy Awards.

[7] ___ Hobson, a Black Businesswoman, investor, and chair of Starbucks.

[8] Mary ___, a former enslaved secret spy for the Union in the Civil War.

Behind the pseudonym "Inkwell Adventures" lies a passionate storyteller and puzzle creator, dedicating their craft to Black history, culture, and heritage magnificence. It isn't just about filling up blank squares or circling letters; it's about embarking on an engaging journey through time, celebrating achievements, acknowledging struggles, and highlighting legends.

Our Mission: We envision a world where Black kids feel proud of their history and are excited to learn and share it. Inkwell Adventures offers a unique opportunity to dive into educational adventures, turning each leisure moment into a learning opportunity. Every word you uncover, every solution you find, and every story you read whispers tales of perseverance, innovation, and resilience.

Our Short Stories: Inkwell Adventures' stories are entertaining, educational, inspiring, and empowering. Focusing on Black children as the main characters, heroes, and heroines, Inkwell Adventures brings creative and inspiring tales that shape young Black minds, boost self-esteem, and offer valuable life lessons. Young black kids will see themselves as the heroes of the stories and relate to them personally as they read about exciting new adventures and fantasy tales that keep them on the edge of their seats. They'll be transported to different worlds and experience new and sensational things that will spark their imagination and inspire them to explore the world around them.

Our Word Games: Each puzzle –a cryptic crossword, a mind-bending scramble, or a vast word search – is a meticulously crafted piece that is more than just a game. Every page beckons young minds to uncover tales of heroes, milestones, art, and revolutions that echo the resounding power of Black voices throughout the ages.

Get Ready to Play and Learn! Prepare to challenge your brain, increase your knowledge, and swell with pride. Whether you're a young learner or simply young at heart, Inkwell Adventures promises hours of educational entertainment. Rediscover history, honor legends, and immerse yourself in the world where word puzzles and short stories transcend mere games and books– they become stories waiting for you to tell.

Thank You for Your Purchase

If you enjoyed this puzzle book,
please consider dropping us a review.

It takes 5 seconds and helps
small businesses like ours.

Use your device's camera to
scan the QR code below.

Made in the USA
Coppell, TX
30 December 2023

27072453R00026